REVERSE COLORING: CITY SKYLINES

Reverse Coloring: City Skylines
ISBN 978-1-961337-10-7

www.SideEyePublishing.com

Welcome to our reverse coloring book, where the rules of coloring are turned upside down, and creativity knows no bounds! We are excited to embark on this unique artistic adventure with you. In this book, you will find vibrant watercolor images that invoke dense city skylines, waiting for your creative touch to bring them to life. Get ready to unleash your imagination and explore a whole new world of artistic expression.

Unlike traditional coloring books, where you color inside the lines, the reverse coloring book challenges you to use your imagination in unexpected ways - adding details and finding worlds inside the colorful shapes. Add as much, or as little detail as you like; create intricate worlds or just doodle around the shapes - this is your opportunity to break the rules and let your artistic intuition guide you.

Here's a helpful tip for using a reverse coloring book: Start by observing the design as a whole before diving in. Take a few quiet moments to study the shapes and the overall composition. Allow your mind to wander and envision the possibilities. Once you're ready, select your tools - pens or pencils - and let your creativity take over. Feel free to explore different techniques, such as varying line thickness, cross hatching, shading, or filling the shapes with intricate patterns and details. Remember, there is no right or wrong way to approach reverse coloring; it's all about embracing the journey and enjoying the process of creating something uniquely yours.

So, welcome to this exciting world of reverse coloring! Let go of expectations, embrace the unexpected, and allow your imagination to run wild. Get ready to turn coloring on its head and uncover a whole new level of artistic expression. We can't wait to see the imaginative creations that will emerge from the pages of this book. Happy reverse coloring!

If you enjoy any of the books in our Reverse Coloring series, please leave a thoughtful review to help others decide if they'd enjoy them too. And if you're looking for other books in the series, or are curious about our other offerings, be sure to check out our Side Eye Publishing page on Amazon.

Thank You!

CREDITS

"abstract-watercolor-brush-strokes-white-paper_2509671"
cover image asset provided by Freepik.com

Made in the USA
Monee, IL
02 December 2023